FAMILY WALKS AROUND EVE[

CONTENTS

ABBREVIATIONS

INTRODUCTION

WALK No 1	HEATH WARREN & LOWER COMMON [4½ miles - 2¼ hours]	4
WALK NO 2	WELSH DRIVE & CASTLE BOTTOM [5 miles - 2½ hours]	6
WALK No 3	EVERSLEY CROSS & UP GREEN [4 miles - 2 hours]	8
WALK No 4	YATELEY COMMON & COUNTRY PARK [3 or 4½ miles - 1½ or 2¼ hours]	10
WALK No 5	LONGWATER & FINCHAMPSTEAD CHURCH [4 miles - 2 hours]	12
WALK No 6	FINCHAMPSTEAD RIDGES & MOOR GREEN LAKES [4½ miles - 2¼ hours]	14
WALK No 7	ROYAL OAK VALLEY & BLACKBUSHE [4½ miles - 2¼ hours]	16
WALK NO 8	HAWLEY LAKE & STARVE ACRE [4½ miles - 2¼ hours]	18
WALK No 9	FARLEY HILL & BLACKWATER RIVER [4½ miles - 2¼ hours]	20

POINTS OF INTEREST   21

MAP SHOWING LOCATION OF WALK STARTING POINTS
and POINTS OF INTEREST   Rear Cover

Published by

FOOTMARK PUBLICATIONS

12 The Bourne, Fleet, Hampshire

FAMILY WALKS SERIES

Family walks around Odiham 1990, 1993

Family Walks around Fleet & Crookham 1991, 1992

Family Walks around Hook & Hartley Wintney 1992

© Footmark Publications 1994. All rights reserved. No part of this publication may be reproduced in any form or by any means (except short passages for review) without the prior written permission of the publisher.

ISBN 0 9515738 4 5   Family Walks around Eversley & Yateley

Great care has been taken to be accurate. The publisher cannot however accept responsibility for any errors which may occur, or their consequences.

All path descriptions have been checked independently, but changes can occur. **If problems are found such as broken or missing stiles and footbridges, barbed wire obstructions, or crops on the path, please contact the Rights of Way Officer asking for the problem to be cleared. Give a map reference if possible. Address & Telephone:**

>   Rights of Way Officer,
>   Basing House,
>   Redbridge Lane,
>   Basing,
>   Basingstoke RG24 0HB   Tel: 0256 29663

ABBREVIATIONS

R	Right	SP	Signpost
RHS	Right hand side	S	Stile
L	Left	FB	Footbridge
LHS	Left hand side	W	Waymark

★ **BOOKBINDING SERVICE**   ~   Repair and restoration

★ **SPECIAL ORDER SERVICE**   ★ **BOOK TOKENS**

★ **TALKING BOOKS**   ★ **BUSINESS & COMPUTER BOOKS**

The Fleet Bookshop

245 Fleet Road, Fleet
Tel: (0252) 616088
Fax: (0252) 812858

INTRODUCTION

This is the fourth book in the Family Walks Series. It covers nine circular walks around Eversley & Yateley of between 4 to 5 miles taking about 2 to 2½ hours at an easy pace. Walks can be started from any point providing the description direction is followed. Numbers on the maps correspond to paragraph numbers in the text. Cars can be parked at starting points shown on the rear cover.

Ordnance Survey Landranger Map 186 shows the paths used, but 2½ inch to the mile Pathfinder Maps show more detail. Readers are encouraged to use these maps and devise their own walks.

Walks pass public houses where food and refreshments are available: The Anchor, Chequers, The Cricketers, Crown & Cushion, Dog and Partridge, The Fox and Hounds, Ely, The Golden Pot, The Greyhound, The Monteagle Arms, Royal Oak, Tally Ho, Le Toad and Stumps, The White Hart and The White Lion.

The walks pass close to many Points of Interest which are described briefly on pages 21 to 24

In dry conditions good walking shoes should suffice, but in wetter conditions wellies may be needed.

Dog owners please keep your dog on a lead where cattle or sheep are grazed to stop it causing injury to livestock or annoyance to other walkers.

Where paths cross fields with crops, the path should be marked by the landowner. Please stick to the line of the path and walk in single file; going round the edge of the field causes damage and is trespassing.

Some walks pass close to private houses - please respect the privacy of residents.

My thanks for help given by: Ted Blackman for the front cover and sketch maps based on out of copyright maps and paths surveys; for checking walks - David Baker, Mark & June Beckley, Paul & Jenny Gibson, Tony & Marianne Morgan, Jim Parker, Pat & Patsy Sansom, Steve & Pam Turner, Hugh & Winifred Warren, John White and Harold Phillips.

                Bob Rose   Fleet   January 1994

WALK No 1   HEATH WARREN & LOWER COMMON

[$2\frac{1}{4}$ hours – $4\frac{1}{2}$ miles]

1. Start from Eversley Church. Go through churchyard, leave by iron gate on enclosed footpath. Cross stile, go along LH field edge, over next stile keeping along LH field edge; cross further stile and follow bank on your R, over stile and take track along edge of wood. At end of field on your R, cross gravel track and continue ahead on track through woods. Shortly before overhead pylon wires, leave track, turn R at wooden posts on path through trees and grass passing gas depot to reach and cross road with care.

1A. NOTE To visit Cudbury Clump, turn L over stile opposite wooden posts noted above, go through new plantation, cross next stile and through tall pines to low mound beside the Welsh Drive. This is Cudbury Clump. Extra return time $\frac{1}{4}$ hour.

2. Enter Bramshill Forest by footpath SP and follow track under pylon wires. Just before wires bear L, look out for and cross stile on R and follow enclosed track. At stile, turn L along gravel drive and then L along New Mill Lane.

3. Just before ford, turn R at metal footpath SP along Blackwater Valley footpath. Cross stile, Turn R into field and cross stile by gate into paddock. At far side of paddock, turn R along enclosed path, cross footbridge, turn L along RH field edge. **Do not cross wooden fence**, but turn L along fence to reach stile. Turn R over stile and cross meadow to further stile. Follow enclosed path to reach The Street, Eversley.

4. Turn R along road – **beware of traffic** – keep on RH side. Just beyond Warbrook at end of wooden barrier, turn R at footpath SP on path through woods passing football field on your L and reach road by The Lodge (beware traffic).

5. Take gravel track opposite to L of Longreach. When track bears R to house, cross two close stiles and keep along LH field edges. Turn L at wire fence, over stile and along RH field edge to enclosed path and return to Eversley Church.

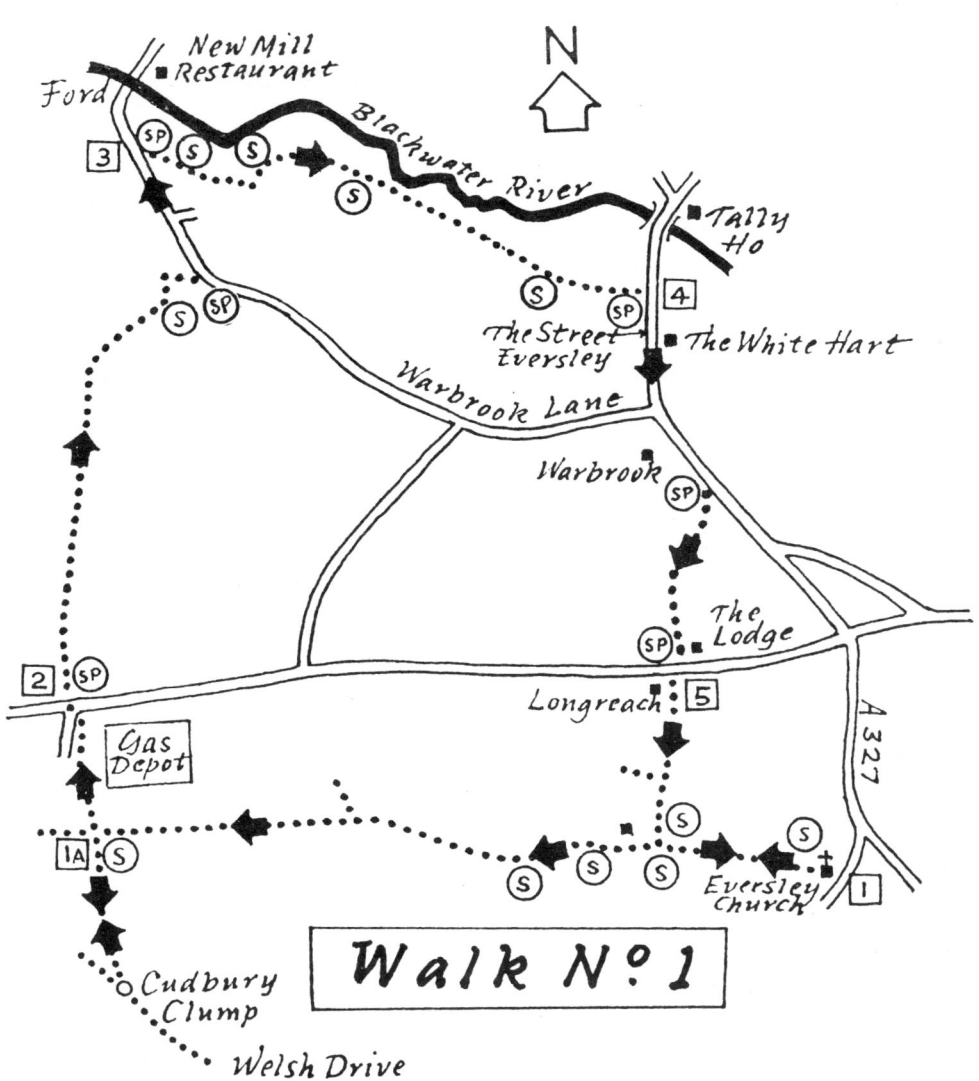

The White Hart

Tel: Eversley 732817
(17th Century Inn on the A327)

Mine Host : **Doug Page**

Real Draught Ales
Fresh Cut Sandwiches
Hot and Cold Snacks Daily
Home-made Country Fare Lunches

Kingsley Barn
~ antiques centre ~

Church Lane, Eversley, Hants
Tel: (0734) 328518

**AFFORDABLE ANTIQUES
QUALITY USED FURNITURE**

Open 6 days a week 10.30am - 5.00pm
Closed Mondays - Except Bank Holidays

WALK No 2   WELSH DRIVE & CASTLE BOTTOM

[5 miles - 2½ hours]

1. Start from Eversley Church. Go along Church Lane to white gates; turn L at footpath SP up track through woods. At top of hill, fork L on track leading to concrete pillar in open space. Turn L along wide gravel track [Welsh Drive] to reach and carefully cross road to bridleway SP opposite. Continue on earth track to cross next road.

2. **Ignore bridleway on the L**; go ahead on gravel track for 200 yards, cross track and turn half L on footpath through trees. It narrows and crosses track, but keep ahead on path through tall pines with gravel workings on your R. At wire fence, turn L along gravel track and shortly cross stile. Follow path through heath; at small clearing, bear R on path descending to Castle Bottom. Cross small stream and ascend with wire fence on your L on path which reaches stile by gate.

3. Cross stile and turn L along stony track (with wooden paling fence on your L); track narrows, then forks L and in 60 yards reaches open space. Turn L on path descending through trees (with wire fence and field on your R) to cross footbridge and stile. Cross field diagonally to stile in opposite corner, continue half L across field towards houses and over stile in corner.

4. Turn R along road; at T-junction by green 'Kits Croft' sign, turn L along road keeping on RH side - **beware traffic**. At cross roads go ahead by 'Except For Access' sign and at T-junction turn R along Chequers Lane. [Note keep along lane to visit The Chequers or Le Toad & Stumps].

5. Shortly by metal footpath SP, turn L along tarmac drive, over stile and along enclosed path with woods on your L. At crossing track, keep along path on LH field edge. At wood corner, turn L along enclosed path by green gate continuing along LH field edge. **Ignore footbridge on your L**, but at corner of field, cross footbridge and stile to enter small field. Follow hedge on your L and shortly turn L along LH field edge to reach and cross stile by metal gate. Turn R along RH field edge and over two stiles. Cross road with great care returning to the church.

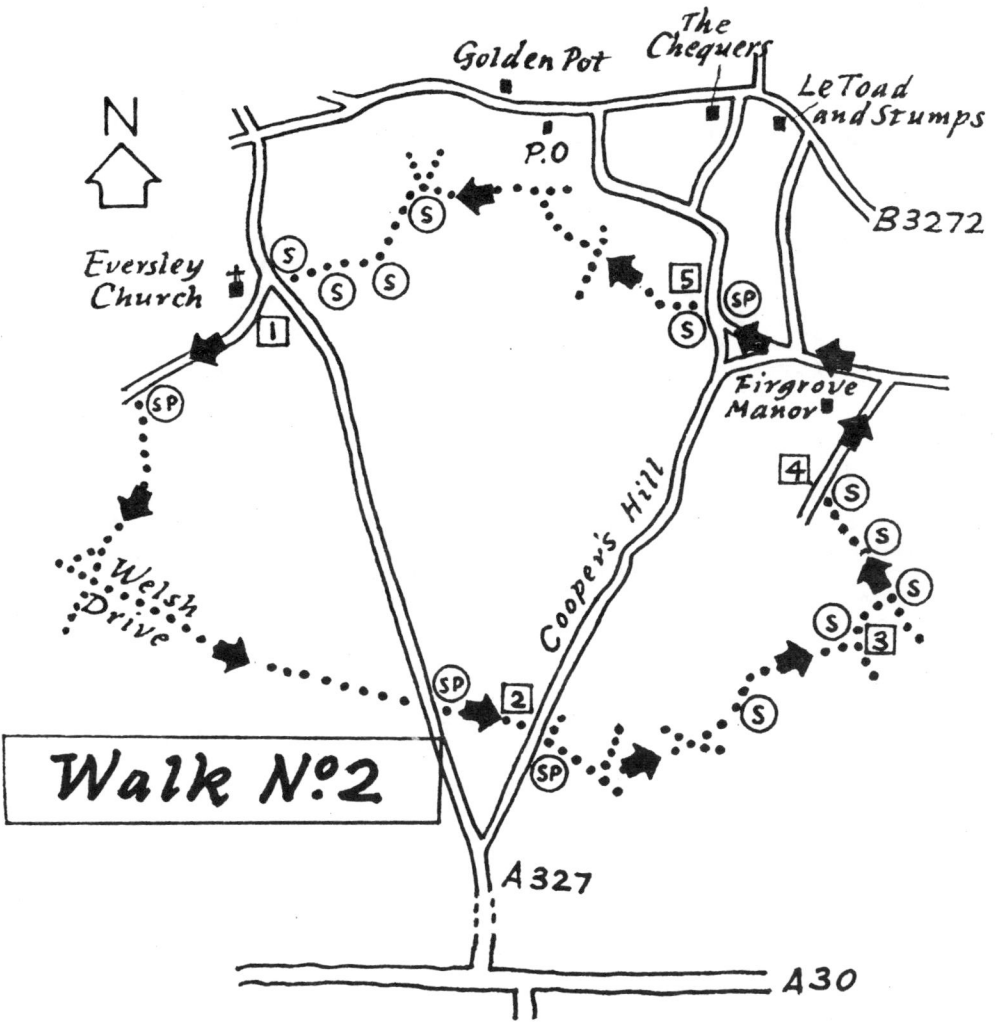

THE GOLDEN POT

Reading Road, Eversley
Tel: 0734 - 732104

Bar Food 12 - 2pm
and Evenings

Bar Games

SOUTHVIEW NURSERIES & GARDEN

Chequers Lane, Eversley Cross

Specialists in old fashioned pinks and hardy herbaceous plants. Half acre plantsmans garden featured in Channel 4 Garden Club

Admission - Nursery free, Garden £1

Open Thurs - Sat 9am - 4.30pm, Feb - Nov.
National Gardens Scheme 2pm - 5pm
on Sunday 12 & 26 June, 1994

WALK No 3   EVERSLEY CROSS & UP GREEN

[4 miles - 2 hours]

1. Start from Cross Green opposite Le Toad & Stumps Bistro. Go along gravel track on LHS of cricket ground, turn R on path in front of pavilions, cross footbridge and stile to enclosed path by stream. Cross two more stiles and bear R along wide track to stile. Turn L along Fox Lane, just beyond Watmore Farm on your L, cross stile on your L by footpath SP and keep along LH field edge to cross stile in corner of field. Turn R then L along wide track between trees. In 50 yards, **do not go through gate ahead**, but turn R along RH field edge to stile in corner. Follow enclosed tarmac path forking R to join Crosby Gardens.

2. Turn R along road and shortly cross with great care B3272 road to byway SP opposite. Go along track leading past Firgrove Farm Cottage. Turn R along RHS of road - **beware traffic**. At cross roads, go ahead by 'Except for Access' sign. At T-junction, turn L along Chequers Lane; just beyond Up Green Farm, look out for footpath SP on your R by gate.

3. Cross stile to path with farm on your R. Cross two adjacent stiles and track, follow RH field edge to footbridge and cross stile. Bear R along RH field edge; at farm gate, take LH of two stiles, go diagonally half L across field to stile in LH corner. [Alternatively use RH stile and go round edge of field with wire fence on your L] Go along LH field edge with trees on your L, cross stile in corner and two footbridges with pond on your R. Cross wire protected by blue hose, go along LH field edges to gate, through Brick House Farm buildings and along drive to road.

4. Turn R along RHS of road - **traffic, take extreme care!** Prior to Eversley Church turning on your L, look out for metal footpath SP in hedge on your R, turn R over stile and go along LH field edges. At corner of second field, turn L over stile by gate and go along RH field edge. At overhead pylon wires, follow hedge round to your R, cross stile and footbridge. Go along RH field edge on enclosed path. At green gate on your L, leave woods on your R, cross field **[not on farm track]** keeping just R of overhead pylon wires. Aim for gap in hedge to L of Hollybush Farm. Go R along lane; at T-junction, turn L along Chequers Lane to The Chequers.

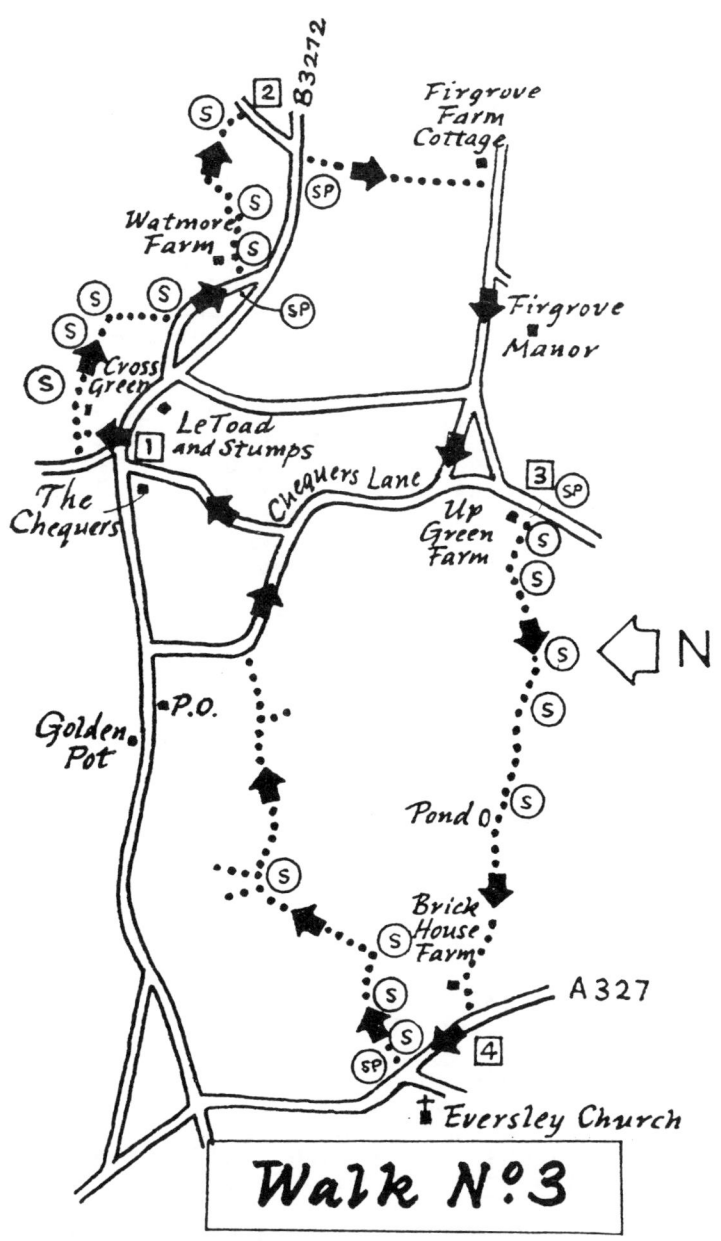

Walk N°3

Le TOAD and STUMPS - EVERSLEY CROSS
"GO NO FURTHER FOR HOMEMADE FOOD"
OPEN ALL DAY   TEL: 0734 - 731126

WALK No 4   YATELEY COMMON & COUNTRY PARK

[3 or 4½ miles - 1½ or 2¼ hours]

1. Start from the public car park behind the Royal Oak. Follow the Royal Oak Valley Footpath with wooden fence on your L. Cross track and continue on enclosed path with wooden fence on your R crossing further track. At open space, cross track and continue on path past The Cricketers on your R. Take path through trees and at bridleway SP, turn L along Handford Lane. Cross Cricket Hill Lane carefully, turn R and shortly at BT box, turn L along track to Wyndham's Pool.

2. Turn R through car park and follow path with pool on your L. Pass Jesse Cottage on your L, **do not take track on your L,** but go ahead on path through trees. At T-junction, turn L along track (note pond to R of junction); shortly turn R on crossing track. Ignore crossing path and go ahead, track bears L at blue waymark post [Note narrow path leads to The Ely].

2A. **Ignore all side turnings in this section.** Pass to R of blue waymark post in clearing by large oaks, continue ahead for 400 yards to pylon. Path shortly descends wide 'steps'; 80 yards on at Y-junction, **do not take RH 'horseshoe' fork**, but fork L with fields on your L to arrive at Strouds Pond. Turn R up wide track to pass Strouds Pond Picnic Area car park on your L.

3. **Ignore 'Residents Only' tracks on your L.** Look ahead and take RH track at Y-junction. At next Y-junction, fork L past blue waymark post; shortly turn R on crossing track to open space with Gravel Pit pond on your R. Keep along LH side of open space to Yateley Country Park map board.

4. Turn L through car park and take path ahead through trees. In 35 yards, turn L at blue waymark post on track through trees. **Ignore all side turnings.** Cross track with Heathfield on your L to track shortly forking L past Cuckoo Cottage. In a few yards, fork R on path through trees, and in 35 yards fork L on path that meanders through trees with field on your L. Path bears R and joins track to pass Cottage Farm on your L.

5. At bridleway SP on your L, turn L along narrow track through trees with fields on your L & R (can be muddy). At T-junction, turn R along wide track to pass Heathlands Cemetery. [To return to Wyndham's Pool, turn L along track opposite cemetery gates] Continue along road, turn L at T-junction and cross Cricket Hill Lane carefully.

6. Go up Beaver Lane, fork R at The Triangle, turn R at crossing track (natural oak seat on your R) and return to the Royal Oak.

Note Shorter walk can be started from any of the car parks passed.

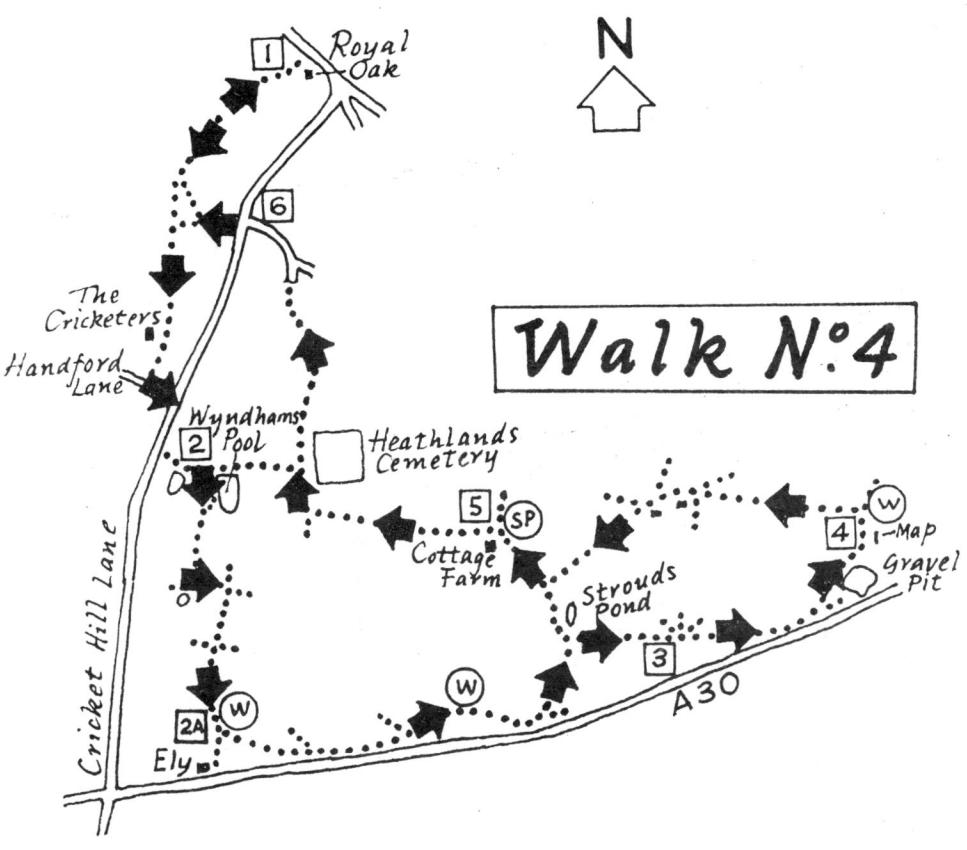

THE CRICKETERS	**ROYAL OAK**
Tel: Yateley (0252) 872105	Tel: Yateley (0252) 872459
Home cooked Food, Lunch & Evening	Mike and Audrey
OPEN ALL DAY	*Food available all day and every day*
Jazz on Wednesday	**MORLANDS REAL ALES**

WALK No 5   LONGWATER & FINCHAMPSTEAD CHURCH

[4 miles - 2 hours]

1. Start from The Tally Ho*, by River Blackwater, Eversley. Turn R up Fleet Hill - **beware traffic**; in 250 yards turn R at footpath SP along lane - marked Blackwater Valley Footpath. Cross stile by farm gate, go along track on LH field edge (with Fleet Copse on your L); at next stile, keep to LH field edge. Cross stile by footpath SP, turn L along enclosed path to join road. [Note Catherine of Aragon plaque on your L by SP]

2. Follow Longwater Lane through houses; at T-junction, cross road and along tarmac track to pass The Greyhound on your R. Turn hard L along road, in 50 yards cross road with care to footpath SP and go up enclosed stoney track/path passing cricket ground on your L. Go up hill, **ignore LH turning at footpath SP**, keep ahead through kissing gate and churchyard to road.

3. Turn L in a few yards at footpath SP along Church Lane past house to enclosed track. Cross drive to Lower Cottage to kissing gate opposite; follow enclosed path between fields.

4. At footpath junction, **take care ignoring stile on your R and other path,** but go through posts to enclosed path on RH field edge with wire fence on your L. Pass wood on your R, continue on enclosed path; cross stile and minor road to kissing gate opposite by footpath SP. Cross field with wire fence on your R to kissing gate opposite. Turn R along road keeping on RHS avoiding traffic and return to The Tally Ho.

* NOTE Ask the Landlord's permission to park

The Tally Ho

Tel: Eversley 0734-732134

David and Shelley welcome you to a traditional village Pub

Real Ale & Good Food available Lunch and Evenings

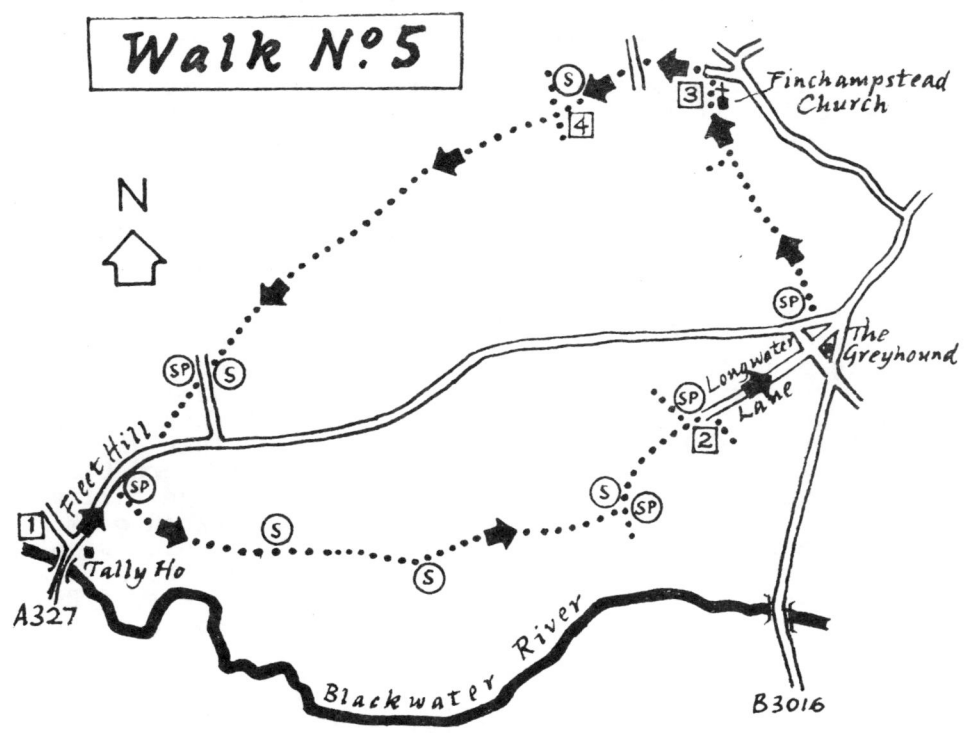

WALK NO 6   FINCHAHPSTAED RIDGES & MOOR GREEN LAKES

[4½ miles - 2¼ hours]

1. Start from Ambarrow Court car park. Cross road with care to footpath SP opposite, follow enclosed path; join road and continue ahead. At Bluebells Farm sign on your R, turn R at footpath SP along track; fork R with field on your L. Ascend through woods, forking R at waymarked post. At T-junction, turn R at bridleway SP along track, **ignore L turn at footpath SP**, but continue to reach and **cross with great care** Wellingtonia Avenue.

2. Turn L along pavement, passing Simons Wood NT car park on your R from which walk can be started. Just before bend in road by Garden Cottage sign on your R, **cross road with extreme caution** to verge opposite and continue to bend in road. **Do not turn L at footpath SP by 'Edge of the Hill' sign**, but bear slightly L at permissive footpath SP across heath. Shortly turn L at waymarked post, descend through woods. At large fallen tree, **do not continue ahead on path at waymarked post**, but turn L passing NT No Horses Beyond This Point sign along path leading to a bar gate. [Note Spout Pond is a few yards along path to your R] After bar gate turn R along track, descend to road at Moor Green House.

3. Turn R along road; in 300 yards opposite Pithers Cottage turn L and, at the far end of the car park, take the enclosed Blackwater Valley Footpath. [Note walk can be started here] At River Blackwater, turn L along riverside path. **Do not cross footbridge over river.** Continue along riverside eventually arriving at Mill Lane.

4. **Do not join Mill Lane**, but turn L through kissing gate, over duckboards following waymarked lakeside path. Go through two kissing gates, **crossing road with care**, to footpath SP opposite. Continue along LH field edges, over stile and through final kissing gate to road. Turn R, **do not enter Yonder**, but immediately at footpath SP, follow path with wooden fence on your L to return to start.

NOTE Walk can be started from Yateley Town Council car park. Go along Moulsham Lane to Moulsham Green. At footpath SP, follow track passing through trees; cross track and continue on enclosed path to footbridge mentioned in paragraph 3.

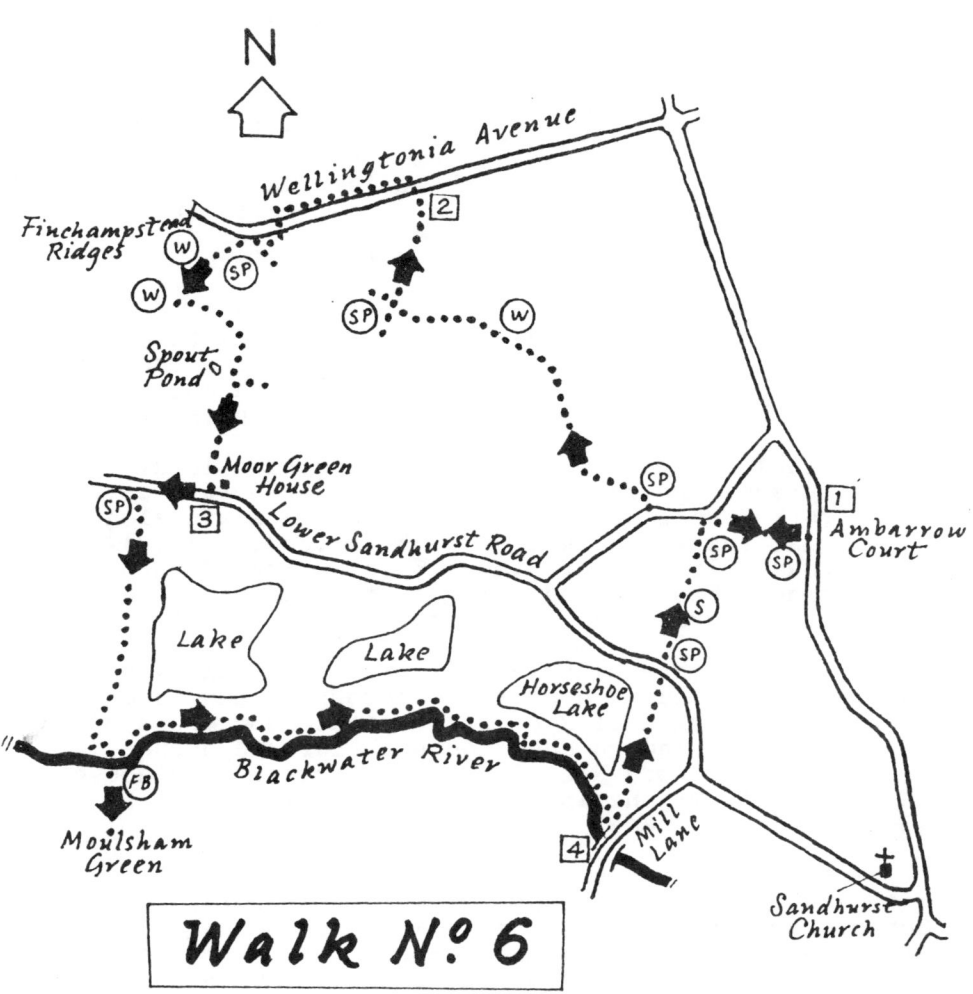

WALK No 7 ROYAL OAK VALLEY & BLACKBUSHE

[4½ miles - 2¼ hours]

1. Start in the public car park behind the Royal Oak from corner opposite CAB. Follow the Royal Oak Valley Footpath with wooden fence on your L. Cross track and continue on enclosed path with wooden fence on your R crossing further track. At open space, cross track and continue on path past The Cricketers on your R. Take path through trees and cross road at bridleway SP.

2. Follow track marked 'Residents Access Only' passing houses on your R; at bridleway SP take track through woods. Turn R along crossing track, soon cross road and follow path past Gas Pipeline post to reach and carefully cross road by junction with Dungells Lane.

3. Continue on track passing horseshoe sign leading to gravel track. **Ignore side turnings**; just before earth bank, fork R on track and shortly turn R again along old tarmac track then R over bank to road. Carefully cross road half R to bridleway SP opposite. Turn L along track through woods, turn L to descend on path (can get overgrown) to The Anchor.

4. Cross road carefully and follow Little Vigo soon turning R. At end of houses, go through green drums and in 25 yards fork half R on grass path. Soon cross old concrete track and go ahead on path through bushes. At end of houses, turn R at drums along track with houses on your R. At T-junction, turn R and immediately L along Monteagle Lane.

5. Pass The Monteagle Arms and continue ahead on road with school playing fields on your R. Turn L along School Lane; at Waitrose, turn R along Monteagle Lane. At roundabout, cross Firgrove Road, through wooden barrier and along enclosed path. After 200 yards, fork R at wooden seat and through two wooden barriers. At concrete bollard go on path through trees which leads to large open grass space. Fork L along path to The Link.
Note Walk can be started from Yateley Town Council nearby.

6. Turn R along road and L at T-junction; shortly fork L on path across Yateley Green. Cross Hall Lane and follow road passing The White Lion on your L and the Dog & Partridge on your R. Go through St Peter's churchyard to tarmac path; in 150 yards, turn L along path between schools. Cross road and continue on wide track opposite. Shortly turn L along narrow path through Royal Oak Valley; at wooden fence, turn L and return to the Royal Oak.

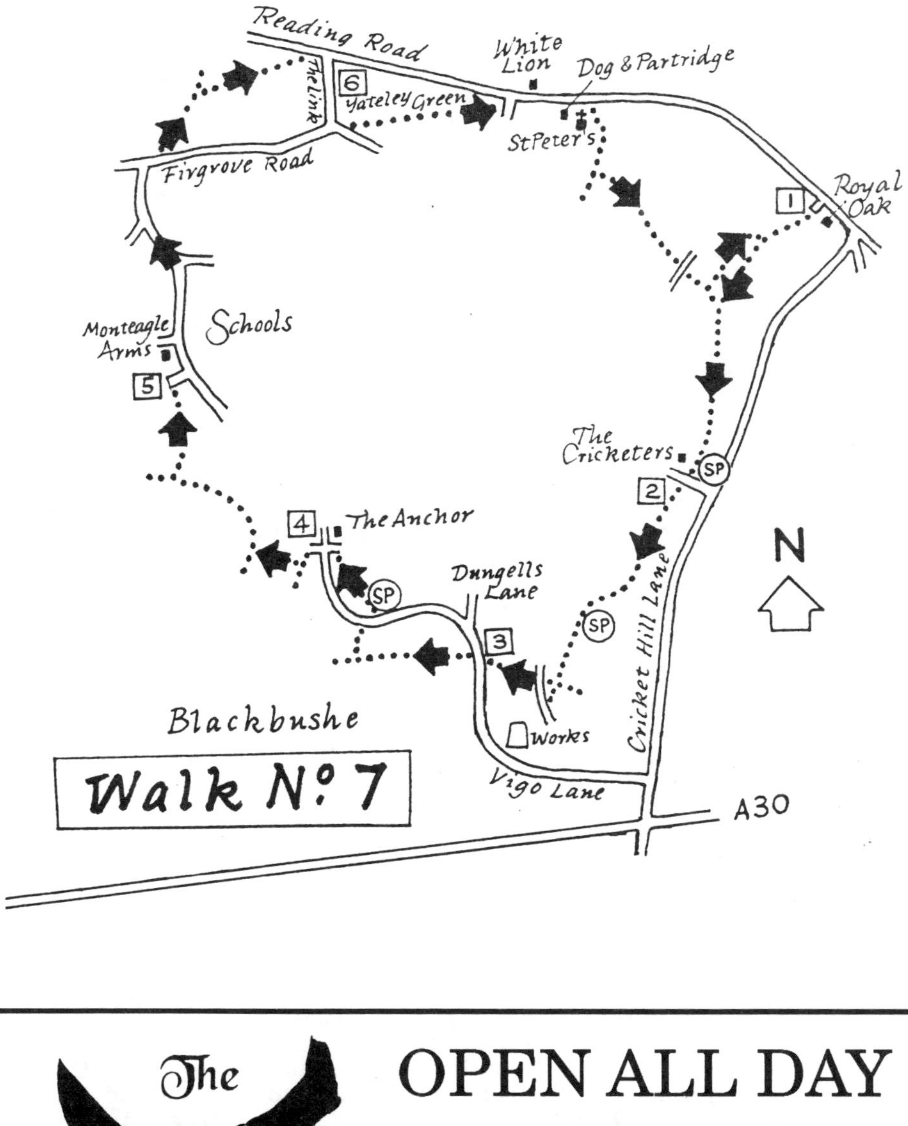
Reading Road
White Lion
Dog & Partridge
The Link
6
Yateley Green
St Peter's
Royal Oak
1
Firgrove Road
Schools
Monteagle Arms
5
The Cricketers
SP
2
4
The Anchor
SP
Dungells Lane
SP
3
Cricket Hill Lane
N
Works
Blackbushe
Vigo Lane
A30
Walk No 7

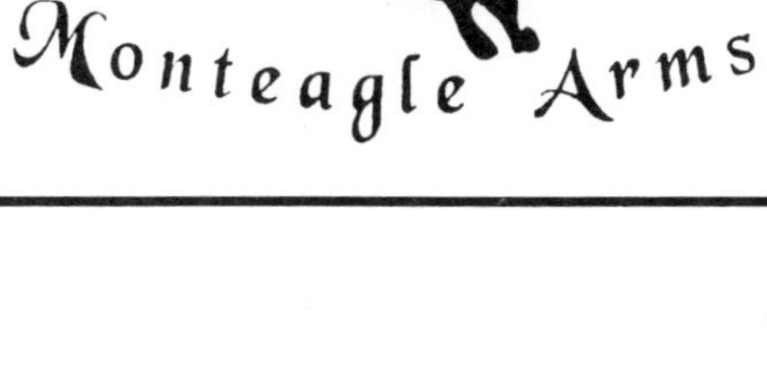

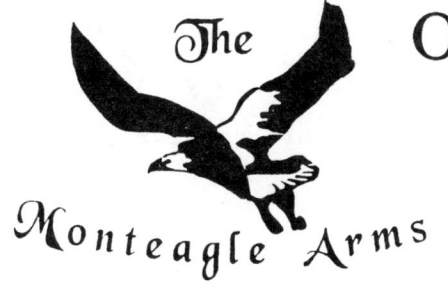

WALK NO 8   HAWLEY LAKE & STARVE ACRE

[4½ miles - 2¼ hours]

1. Start from Hawley Memorial Hall, Hawley Green. Turn L out of car park and immediately L on enclosed path through rhododendrons. Turn L along wide gravel track; after ¼ mile at wooden pylons, fork R on sandy/stony track. At top of hill, **ignore side turnings** and fork L; becomes gradual descent, **still ignore side turnings**. Cross made-up track and continue on sandy track opposite.

2. Turn L along tarmac road; shortly at next junction, keep ahead on road leading to side gate by main gate. Pass boat yard and Hawley Hard RE Yard on your L. Keep on road for ¼ mile.

3. At 'BFT ROUTE 1 MILE' sign, leave road turning L past gate onto gravel track. After 300 yards, side turning on your R leads to Crown & Cushion, **but keep on main track** shortly forking L. **Ignore next turn on R**; in about 100 yards at blue waymark post on your R, turn L onto earth path and R in 100 yards at next blue waymark on your L close by a 'Sewerage Main' post (path can be muddy). Cross bridge with concrete parapet, keep along sandy edge of lake; follow path through trees.

4. At tarmac road, turn L over bridge with brick parapet; in a few yards leave road, turn R and immediately L at blue waymark posts, go on earth track with wire fence on your L and houses on your R. Turn L at blue waymark along crossing track continuing ahead past two further blue waymark onto tarmac road. At T-junction leave road, go ahead on earth track. At next T-junction, turn L and in a few yards R on stony track. Keep ahead uphill **ignoring side turnings**.

5. At top of hill, turn L at blue waymark post along tarmac road and, in a few yards just past gatepost at T-junction and next blue waymark, turn R along road. Shortly before wooden barrier, bear half R at wooden pylons and follow track under overhead wires. In 400 yards this joins track with rhododendrons on your L. Track becomes enclosed and descends; in 500 yards joins wide gravel track. In about 25 yards, bear R at waymark on path through rhododendrons and return to start.

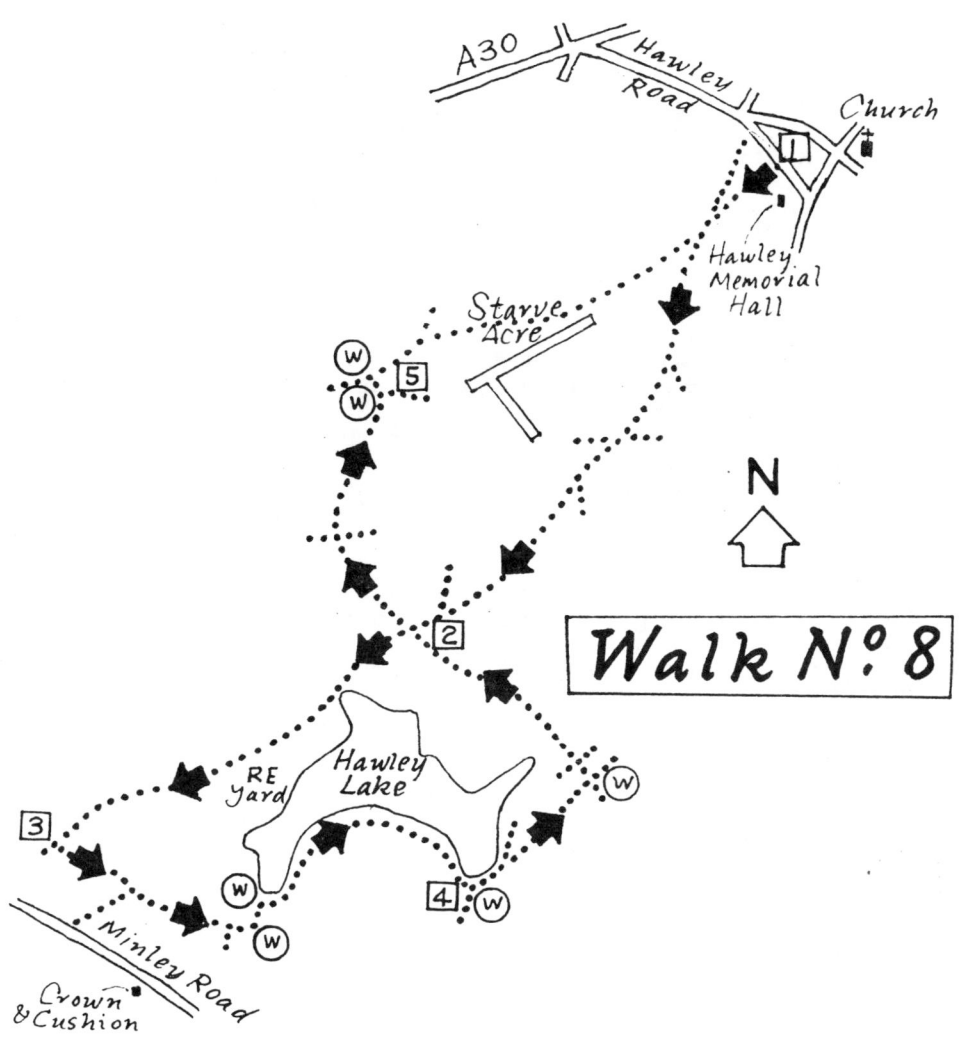

WALK No 9   FARLEY HILL & BLACKWATER RIVER

[4½ miles - 2¼ hours]

1. Start at the Fox & Hounds*, Farley Hill; cross side lane, just beyond Brockendene at footpath SP, turn R along enclosed path. At fence, turn R along bottom of garden then L along enclosed path. Turn R over stile, along RH field edge, turn L over stile and through woods. At next stile, go straight ahead across field aiming for footpath SP to the L of pylon. Bear slightly R along LH side of line of trees, cross stile and footbridge and follow path through woods.

2. Cross stile and field diagonally R to stile opposite. Go along RH field edge, at corner of field by white house, turn R along track. Turn R along road, fork R and pass Greenacres Farm. At footpath SP, go ahead on track, turn R at wooden fence over stile along enclosed footpath - marked Blackwater Valley Footpath. Shortly turn R over stile at footpath SP, cross field to stile in opposite LH corner. Continue along LH field edge; at the third stile, turn L along LH field edge to pass Jouldings Farm.

3. At footpath SPs, cross road and stile opposite, go along LH field edges by river, crossing stiles to reach road at Thatcher's Ford. Cross road and stile continuing by riverside. **Do not cross river footbridge.** Shortly pass confluence of Blackwater & Whitewater. By overhead cables, turn R over stile, along enclosed path and turn R at stile along road.

4. Turn L at T-junction; 350 yards on at top of hill, look out for footpath SP on your L, ascend steps and along LH field edge. At wooden sleeper, cross field and continue along road. At T-junction, turn R and cross road with care to drive opposite, bear half L along drive and track beside Village Hall & Church. Turn R along road and L along Church Road to return to Fox & Hounds.

* NOTE Ask the Landlord's permission to park

~ THE FOX AND HOUNDS ~

Rodney and Lesley Clark

BAR FOOD and MEALS ~ OPEN 11am to 11pm
LARGE GARDEN

Church Road, Farley Hill.   Tel **(0734) 733266**

POINTS OF INTEREST

Eversley

Castle Bottom is the site of former cottages on Eversley Common, but little trace remains of them. It is a surprisingly isolated hollow of ancient heathland near to Blackbushe Airfield. Traces of a low round tumulus were said to be obliterated by airfield works. It was on the main dyke boundary of Crondall Manor confirmed by King Edgar in 975. The name derives from the mai or main meaning castle in Celtic. A bank along the parish boundary to the present A30 was made by Militia encamped locally in 1803.

[Walk No 2]

The Church of Blessed Mary the Virgin There was a church on the site by 1294. The chancel was built about 1500; in 1724 the whole church, west of the chancel screen, was re-built by John James. The tower was completed in 1736. In 1876 the church was 'restored' as a memorial to Charles Kingsley, rector from 1844 until his death in 1875. He was a social reformer, naturalist, author of The Water-Babies, but probably most importantly a simple, well-loved, parish priest. He was buried beside the avenue of yews he planted in the churchyard.

[Walk Nos 1, 2 & 3]

Cross Green Eversley's ancient origins are suggested by the village sign erected on the green commemorating Queen Elizabeth's Silver Jubilee in 1975. Eversley may be derived from "Efor Leigh" or field of the wild boar. It is one of the few remaining records of the existence of wild boar in England. The cricket ground on the green is the venue of an annual benefit match with Hampshire.

[Walk No 3]

Firgrove Manor   Wadham Wyndham prospered in the service of the South Sea Company and this, together with a dowry of £8000 on marrying his cousin Catherine, enabled him early in the 18th century to build Firgrove Manor - possibly by John James. It may occupy the site of an earlier building or monastery. The Wyndhams were a Saxon family of nobility originally from Norfolk. They were one of the two leading families in Yateley and strong supporters of the Jacobites in southern England. Wadham Wyndham was a well-known amateur coachman.
[Walk Nos 2 & 3]

New Mill dates from 1577 when it replaced an earlier mill destroyed by fire. The Domesday Book records two mills in the vicinity. For over 300 years New Mill was owned by the St John family who rented it to the Spencers. A later tenant, Mr Wescott, added the lock bridge and started a saw mill. Local farmers brought corn to the mill for grinding until earlier this century. New Mill is a listed building and has been a restaurant since 1972. The waterwheel and corn grinding equipment are still in working order.
[Walk No 1]

Warbrook House was built in 1724 by the architect John James for himself. Despite recent additions, the period building has survived virtually intact. The grounds were laid out using the principles of Dezallier d'Argenville; James translated the French treatise. The West front of Warbrook House has a breath-taking view down the tree-lined canal which exemplifies his mastery of landscaping. James was born in 1672 at Stratfield Turgis, educated at Basingstoke and apprenticed to Matthew Bankes, the King's Carpenter. He became a architect and, as a colleague of Sir Christopher Wren, was involved in the completion of St Paul's Cathedral where he held was Surveyor to the Fabric. He designed many other buildings in London after the Great Fire in 1666 and also a number of buildings in Hampshire. His achievements are recorded on a memorial tablet in Eversley Church.
[Walk No 1]

The Welsh Drive is an old drovers' road used to take cattle from Wales and the West Country to London. This stopped when the railways developed. An annual fair was held on 8 November at Blackwater. The Welsh Drive passes close to Cudbury Clump a Bronze Age burial barrow.
[Walk Nos 1 & 2]

Finchampstead

Catherine of Aragon   In 1501 Prince Arthur, eldest son of Henry VII, started out from Windsor Castle to meet his fiancee Catherine of Aragon. He was met at Finchampstead by her guardians. The meeting spot is marked by a plaque. Against royal Spanish custom, Prince Henry rode on to meet her at Dogmersfield. A dance was held there in the evening.
[Walk No 5]

Finchampstead Ridges is National Trust property and provides a fine viewpoint to the south across the Blackwater Valley and parts of Berkshire, Hampshire and Surrey. Just to the north, the London to Silchester Roman Road called the Devil's Highway crosses Simons Wood. Wellingtonia Avenue is an outstanding half mile avenue of a hundred giant Sequoia trees, native to North America, planted in 1863 in memory of the Duke of Wellington.
[Walk No 6]

Moor Green Lakes are a nature reserve restored from former gravel pits. Habitats have been created for a wide variety of birds. They can be seen from the Blackwater Valley Footpath.
[Walk No 6]

Parish Church of St James retains the walls of the original church built about the time of the Norman Conquest. The Normans elaborated the simple Saxon church to its more or less present form in 1150. The font is the original - credited 1030. About 1375 a small chapel was added on the north side removing part of the Norman wall. The chapel was extended about 1475 and a corner entrance constructed in 1590. The red brick tower built in 1720; it has six bells, five dating from 1792. A list of rectors from 1299 is in the 19th century porch.
[Walk No 5]

Hawley

Crown & Cushion has associations with Colonel Thomas Blood who lived at Minley Warren. In 1671 he nearly succeeded in stealing the Crown Jewels from the Tower of London. Although he escaped, he was later arrested whilst imbibing in the Crown & Cushion. This was commemorated by a topiary in front of the pub cut in the shape of a crown on a cushion, sadly no longer trimmed. Blood was granted a Royal Pardon and an estate in Ireland worth £500 a year. Who said crime does not pay!
[Walk No 8]

Hawley Lake in Hawley Common is a popular walking, sailing and fishing area. The Common was part of the Minley Manor grounds owned by the Currie family, local benefactors who gave land for the cricket pavilion by Hawley Green and later for the Hawley War Memorial Hall. The lake and surrounding common are now used by the Royal Engineers as a training area and walkers should keep to paths.
[Walk No 8]

Sandhurst

Ambarrow Court was built in 1885 for Colonel Harvey from designs by the architect F Ravenscroft; it was surrounded by over 21 acres of woodland. On his widow's death, it was offered for sale in 1932 by Messrs Nicholas of Reading for use as a school, nursing home or institution. In Autumn 1940 it was requisitioned as an outstation of Radio Department, Royal Aircraft Establishment following the bombing of RAE Farnborough in August 1940. The house was then empty, but contained much German literature which lends credence to rumours that it had been used for interrogation of enemy agents. After it was relinquished by RAE in 1969, it became derelict and the house was demolished. Fortunately the weather-cock has been preserved on a building in RAE. The grounds, once a 'secret garden', are now open to the public as is adjacent Ambarrow Hill.
[Walk No 6]

Yateley

Blackbushe In the Second World War, RAF Hartford Bridge airfield was built on common land crossed by The Welsh Drive. The road over the common to Vigo Lane has never been re-opened. One runway crossed the A30 and traffic was diverted onto the Fleet Road. It was first used by Aerodynamics Flight, Royal Aircraft Establishment testing gliders later used at D-Day. A variety of operational squadrons used the airfield including: RCAF Tomahawks, RAF photographic reconnaissance Spitfires, RAF & Free French Bostons bombers and Polish Mosquitos. Shot-up returning aircraft could use emergency landing strips at Starve Acre [Walk No 8] on Hawley Common. Blackbushe had FIDO — fog dispersal system. There is a memorial plaque at the airfield honouring aircrew lost in action .
[Walk No 7]

St Peter's Parish Church is built on the site of a Saxon church said to have been burnt down about 750. The earliest record of the church is in the Domesday Book (1080); there is a roll of incumbents back to 1226. The north wall from behind the wooden font to the organ is Saxon and was extended to its present length about 1100. The chancel was completed by 1220 and the wooden tower about 1500. The church was burnt down in 1979 leaving only the walls, charred timbers of the tower and cracked bells — the oldest cast in 1577. It was rebuilt by 1981. The chancel became the chapel and contains the 13th century font; the clock originally 1600 was restored.
[Walk No 7]

Yateley Common Country Park is one of the few remaining heathlands in North East Hampshire. It was originally cleared of forest in the Bronze Age for crops & livestock. The poor soil was soon exhausted and colonized by plants such as heather and gorse. For hundreds of years it was kept open by commoners cutting fuel & turf and continuous grazing. As this declined, birch and pine invaded the Common. This has been reversed by Country Park Rangers' careful management. The Common has several ponds. Stroud Pond was recorded in the Domesday Book as a fish pond; stakes to prevent poaching have been traced. Wyndhams Pool is named after a local family.
[Walk No 4]